FRANCE

SMITHMARK

Text
Simonetta Crescimbene

Graphic design
Patrizia Balocco

Contents

2-3 Orderly rows of grape vines stretch along the hillsides of Alsace, near Riquewihr. In autumn, these villages are the setting for festivals and celebrations.

4-5 French architecture has always been daring and ambitious. Over the centuries, the styles have changed, but the spirit remains the same - a spirit that is perfectly expressed in I.M. Pei's glass pyramid in the courtyard of the Louvre, in Paris. The structure stands over 70 feet tall, and manages to harmonize with the style of the older building, dating back centuries.

6 Sainte-Chapelle was built as a shrine in which to store a relic believed to be Christ's crown of thorns, and other relics now kept in the treasure of Notre-Dame. The upper chapel - there are two, one set atop the other - is almost entirely made of windows, in a spectacular example of architectural precision.

7 Notre Dame, a masterpiece of Gothic architecture, built between 1163 and 1250, underwent further modifications in later centuries. Today, visitors can visit the setting of the adventures of Quasimodo, the hunchback, and Esmeralda, as described by Victor Hugo, or improvise a merry outing among grotesques and gargoyles, as restored by the architect Viollet-le-Duc.

8-9 The light and colors of Saint-Tropez attracted many painters. Signac, Matisse, Bonnard, Marquet, and Dunoyer de Segonzac flocked here, while such writers as Maupassant and Colette were seduced by the charm of the venerable pastel facades of the buildings in the old harbor.

10-11 The most sought-after oysters are those caught off the Atlantic coast, much prized by gourmets. In the Morbihan, in Brittany, fishing is a local mainstay.

This edition published in 1994 by SMITHMARK Publishers Inc., 16 East 32nd Street, New York, NY 10016.

SMITHMARK books are available for bulk purchase for sales promotion and premium use. For details write or call the Manager of Special Sales, SMITHMARK Publishers InC., 16 East 32nd Street, New York, NY 10016; (212) 532-6600.

First published by Edizioni White Star. Title of the original edition: Francia, la douceur du vivre. © World copyright 1993 by Edizioni White Star. Via Candido Sassone 22/24,13100 Vercelli, Italy.

ISBN 0-8317-3371-3

Printed in Singapore by Tien Wah Press Color separations by Magenta, Lit. Con., Singapore.

Introduction

Mirabeau, Fontenay-aux-Roses, Rochefort, Fleurance, Les Sables-d'Olonne, Pont Saint-Esprit… just the sound of French place names is sufficient to evoke images of still lakes, lush gardens, and fairy-tale cottages. Modern readers, however, may be more familiar with terms to describe environmental catastrophe, unscrupulous development, and rogue industrialization. We are almost reluctant to believe that a wise government could protect the pastoral beauty of the French countryside.

And so, as a visitor crosses the French border, there is a considerable temptation to wander at large; to eliminate, somehow, distances and obstacles; in brief, to take in at one glance the whole of the nation — the shimmering chalk cliffs of Étretat, the geological curiosities of the Puys mountains, the vast scented fields of lavender and rosemary in the Garrigues — so that no single wonder or marvel can elude one's gaze. Before the infinite variety of France, the visitor is disarmed. It is hard to say which is more overwhelming: the abundance and loveliness of the landscape, or the wealth of the past. History seems to leap out from every corner, posturing and declaiming — in the form of urban graffiti or dashing Impressionist brushstrokes, Gothic spires or modern cantilevers, the cave paintings of Lascaux or the grand arch of La Défense outside Paris.

It is perhaps no accident that we have borrowed the term "avant-garde." Throughout history, in every circumstance and juncture, the French have broken the chains of tradition and given free rein to innovation and creativity; they have done so in settings that range from the chilly garrets of the Bohemians to the monumental splendor described in French as "la grandeur." In the student revolts of May 1968, "L'imagination au pouvoir" (roughly, "power to the imagination") was a slogan chanted outside the Sorbonne; in a sense, however, it is a venerable motif of French culture.

Intuitive leaps can be just as important in technological progress as the most painstaking calculations. The visionary genius of Jules Verne

provides an adequate demonstration of this adage, as does the pioneering photography and cinematography of Jacques Daguerre and the Frères Lumière, who triggered a revolution in modern culture by broadening the horizons of artistic media. And nowadays, the films of René Clair, Jean Cocteau, Claude Chabrol, François Truffaut, Louis Malle, and Jean-Luc Godard occupy an honored place in the annals of cinema; they communicate to the rest of the world an authentic flavor of French esprit. That esprit — or spirit — has a special meaning to a great many people; it evokes France, but it also evokes a period of their lives. It summons up memories of bitter-voiced poets, philosophers, and café singers, denouncing the nausea and ennui of modern life. It recalls the existential travail of an entire generation of European intellectuals. Yet it also evokes the rustle of silk and chiffon, luxurious fashion shows in vintage newsreels, and the first glimmerings of the hedonistic age of Haute Couture. France is, in short, a hotbed of new ideas; often the French succeed in turning these ideas into "trends" that sweep the world.

This nation, ever youthful and new, possesses a remarkable equilibrium, a fine balance between daring and tradition, between the spectacular and the understated. There is a solid and versatile culture tucked away in the heart of each region. Part of the challenge — and joy — of touring France is to discover these separate traditions. An imaginative visitor, for instance, may choose to spend time drifting along the placid canals of Burgundy. This canal network, built centuries ago, is the best known one in France, but from Normandy to Provence, there are numerous other wonderful river and canal routes, navigable by barge. The barges, or "péniches," ply the river currents at a steady five knots, trailing streams of ripples and wavelets. At this leisurely pace, the passengers can enjoy the verdant landscape as it creeps by, reflected in the mirroring water. In a succession of locks, these waterways link the most important rivers in France — the Seine, the Loire, the Rhône, and the Saône become paths along which one can set out to explore the homeland of the ancient Gauls, here and there unchanged through millennia of history. And, if the charms of nature are not sufficient to soothe the soul, there are the charms of French dining. Entrancing riverfront villages with evocative names welcome the amateur sailor; here one can dock directly at restaurants serving such local specialties as chicken flambé à la moutarde or pain d'épice dijonnais, liberally accompanied by a fine dry chablis or a white mâcon. The Côte d'Or possesses two wine-growing regions: the Côte de Nuits in the north and

14

the Côte de Beaune in the south. In this area, during the summer, both locals and well-informed visitors stroll along the illuminated rows of the vineyards until late into the night. Illustrious vineyards and venerable "caves," or vintners, dot the landscape, amidst a profusion of colorful gardens and delicate pergolas, stately bell towers and medieval villages, and cool groves of plane and chestnut trees. Everywhere one sees evidence of the loving pride of the residents. Perhaps the most fitting representative of this region is the "éclusier," or lock-keeper, who courteously ushers the barge through the hydraulic machinery of the locks with the same traditional motions and gestures used by his father and his grandfather before him. While waiting for the barge to rise or settle to the level of the stream ahead, a visitor should take advantage of the lock-keeper's lore. He may describe some of the remarkable architectural and historical treasures of the region, often overlooked by travelers.

Among the monuments those travelers overlook are no fewer than 350 Romanesque churches. Cluny, with its renowned Benedictine abbey, was the cornerstone of the Burgundian Romanesque school of building, a style that spread over all of Europe. All over the region, small towns and villages still possess vestiges of this great architectural revolution. The countryside abounds, therefore, in fairy-tale landscapes, spellbinding at times; one can sense the excitement of artistic innovation that must have swept this region ten centuries before, without ever having to leave the comfort of the barge, with its comfortable deck and the gentle pitch, yaw, and roll of the "maison," or cabin. This is French living at its most carefree.

This charmed union between earth and water may serve as a fitting prologue to another, equally bewitching region: Brittany. Here, in bracing contrast with the quiet, enameled waters of Burgundy, rough Atlantic waves crash foaming onto the red granite rocks of the northern coast of the Breton peninsula. This last strip of land, stretching out into the mighty ocean, is called Finistère, a name taken from the .Latin "finis terrae," which means 'end of the world.' On this stark backdrop, nature rages; here, pirates once roamed the coasts, looting and laying waste on shore and at sea. Now brigantines and galleons have been replaced by fishing floats, hull down on the horizon under a changing, lowering sky. The tangy and pungent aroma of the waves hovers over shoals, reefs, and islets, which disappear and resurface with the cadenced surge of the tides.

Over millennia, the waves have painstakingly carved away at the rocky shores, studded with seashells and crabs. The intricate coastline is a perfect vantage point from which to observe the ocean, in all of its timeless mystery.

The ebb and flow of the water is a perfect correlary to the lives led here. This tenacious, stubborn people, with a language and a past perhaps more closely linked to Britain than to continental France, seems to have modeled itself on the sea. The Bretons are oceanfarers, deeply marked by the awareness of life's fragility in the face of stern nature. They are proud of all they have survived; after waves of invaders — first Roman armies, and then Celtic and Frankish settlers — Brittany became an independent dukedom, a rank it defended until the inevitable surrender to growing French might in 1532. Despite the loss of political independence, the region remained culturally and artistically distinct, and some folkways are intact today. In small towns it is not rare to see knots of matrons commenting, in Breton dialect, on the Sunday sermon, their hair adorned with the intricate and traditional lace headgear. These spotless white folds of lace are worn on the numerous religious and town feastdays, such as the blessing of the fishing nets, which takes place in Concarneau in the month of August.

From May to September, during the so-called "pardons," the visitor has the best opportunity, however, to explore the Breton spirit, which imbues the largest towns as profoundly as it does the most remote village. These processions are the latter-day version of feasts held to honor the Virgin and all of the saints; the Church once granted plenary indulgence to all the faithful on those occasions. A deep-seated mysticism and austere customs are — and were, in Celtic tradition — traits that link Armor, the maritime section of Brittany, with Argoat, the inland region, countrified and heavily wooded. The distinctive "enclos parroissiaux," or walled squares surrounding the church, and the unsettling figures of the "calvaries," gazing out at us across centuries of medieval gloom, are eloquent of an ancient spirituality. Ossuaries, cemeteries, chapels, and fountains have been monuments of Christian inspiration through the centuries, but one of the most peculiar monuments in Brittany is equally religious — the megaliths of Carnac. One's first impression upon entering the plain of Ménec is that of being overwhelmed by the thousands of colossal upright stones, standing in circular or rectangular array or, here and there, in solitary majesty. It is believed that these stones were erected by sun-worshiping peoples who dwelt here in the third and second millennia B.C. These gigantic primitive temples stand witness to the

12-13 The Côte d'Or is the wide area in Bourgogne where excellent wines such as Beaujolais and Chablis are produced. It is divided into two areas: the Côte de Nuits in the North, famous for the red wines of Nuits St. Georges, Chambolle-Musigny, Morey St. Denis, and the Côte de Beaune, where such white and red wines as Pommard, Auxey-Duresses, St.-Romain, and Volnay are produced.

14-15 A golden field of sunflowers, seemingly boundless in this picture, shows the inspiring Provençal landscape, which Van Gogh reproduced majestically during his stay at Arles.

16 top These proud pines stand in the national park of Ecrins, located in the Dauphiné. The park's highest points are Mount Pelvoux and the Barre des Écrins; in this remarkable protected area one can hike, climb, or cycle.

16 bottom La Vallouise, a river valley carved out by the Durance, is a pleasant route to Briançon. Equidistant from the national park of Écrins and the wilderness of Queyras, this is a perfect staging area for a number of hikes.

17 The Atlantic Pyrenees slope gently down to the ocean. The steady sunlight from May on makes trekking from one high valley to another particularly enjoyable.

18-19 If one follows the Seine to the ocean, one reaches Honfleur. This small and handsome port, crowded with buildings dating from the sixteenth and seventeenth centuries, looks much as it did when its homes were built.

unimaginable efforts these peoples were willing to lavish in order to exalt the glory of their god. The sight of these stones at sunset, their long shadows creeping across the earth, is impressive and memorable. Menhirs, dolmens, châteaux, and chapels — all are built of the same hard grey granite, as if every single thing had petrified at the dawn of creation. Inland, the lush green of the forests is broken at intervals by the deep blue of the canals, mirroring the solid granite houses with their sharply pitched blue-grey stone roofs.

This enchanting landscape, dotted with venerable mills, can be seen in the paintings of the artists of Pont-Aven, chief among them Paul Gauguin. It is scarcely surprising that these artists should have given up Paris, seeking inspiration amidst the poetic nature of Brittany. The region attracted writers as well as painters — Guy de Maupassant and Guillaume Apollinaire lived here. Again, little wonder, considering Brittany's ancient literary tradition — this is the setting for the medieval legends of King Arthur. In the so-called Dark Ages, the forest of Brocéliande extended across the Breton heartland, offering imaginary haven to such fabled characters as Lancelot and the sorcerer Merlin.

The year 1000, which marked the dawn of a new millennium, was a turning point in what is now France. In just three centuries, dozens of cathedrals and hundreds of churches sprang up across the land. In those days, everyone lent a hand in the construction of religious buildings — some offered manual labor, so as to atone for past sins with the sweat of their brows; others offered funds in exchange for dispensations. It was through the latter system of exchange that the town of Rouen, in Normandy, obtained a flamboyant Gothic masterpiece, La Tour du Beurre, or The Tower of Butter. This remarkable construction was financed by the townspeople in exchange for ecclesiastic authorization to eat butter during Lent. Whatever the circumstances, however, the profusion of new churches and cathedrals was an expression of a great and widely felt passion. Medieval mysticism launched the imaginations of builders and architects upward, in a heaven-bent crescendo of aspiration that took the form of tapering arches, Gothic vaults, flying buttresses, and towering spires and pinnacles. Towers and belfries attained dizzying heights; stone was rendered light and airy by oculi, fretworks, and rose windows as intricate as the finest lace. Particolored stained-glass windows brought shafts of light through the massive walls, while statues of saints, devils, and grotesque monsters adorned the exterior. These buildings sprang up across all of what is now France, but they were especially plentiful in Ile-de-France and Normandy.

Normandy, in particular, boasts the churches and cathedrals of Evreux, Rouen, Fécamp, Lisieux, Caen, Bayeux, Coutances, and Mont-Saint-Michel; the latter abbey stands on the border with Brittany, and in some sense links the two regions. Nature and history have conspired to make Mont-Saint-Michel unlike anything else on earth — set amidst an expanse of ever-changing sands which are illuminated by the restless coastal light and flooded at regular intervals by the most powerful tides in Europe, the island-abbey rears up, a startling metaphor for medieval society. Tourists flock to this portion of the Norman coastline, and many take the opportunity for a stroll across the tidal sands, enjoying some of the most spectacular views of the mount. Before doing so, however, it is wise to know just when the next high tide is expected. The waters rise rapidly, driving up the level of rivers and surrounding and engulfing the sandy shoals.

Normandy abounds in vernacular architecture; the "maison à colombage," or "dovecote house," is particularly typical of the old section of Rouen. This style of construction varied freely from the Middle Ages to the Renaissance; the houses are, in turn, distinguished by sharp angles, straight lines, or steep pitches, squat or soaring, ostentatious or understated; wooden half-beams mark the facade. Gustave Flaubert was originally from Normandy, and these houses serve as backdrops in many of his novels, including *Madame Bovary.*

Normandy's splendid Gothic stained glass, meant to elevate the spirit in mystical ecstasy, and the Normandy's excellent literature, designed to revolutionize the novel, must share pride of place with yet another of the region's "creations," perhaps less noble, but equally vital to life here — Norman cider. The region is covered with vast orchards in which no fewer than seventy different varieties of apple tree flower each May, overwhelming the visitor with color and aroma. And in October, when the rest of France is busy harvesting grapes, the apple trees of Normandy are bowed down with ripe fruit. This is the time to visit the cider "vintners," to taste the aromatic fruit juice. Some of this juice, each year, will be distilled into the lively local eau-de-vie, Calvados.

Normandy reaped another, less joyful harvest — during the massive Allied invasion in June of 1944. The damage done by bombardment and shelling can still be seen here and there, and there are vast cemeteries where soldiers of all nationalities rest in eternity. And even these fields of stone and greensward can become tourist attractions, particularly

if a well-known name appears on a headstone.

Likewise, the Parisian cemeteries of Père-Lachaise, Montmartre, and Montparnasse are pleasant spots in which to stroll, along lanes crowded with marble angels, stone muses, and baroque curlicues, dangling in silence. Paul Valéry, in "Cimetière marin," based on the graveyard of Sète, wrote, "...La vie est vaste, étant ivre d'absence," roughly, "Life is vast here, drunk with absence..." And the tourists and visitors come in great numbers, to pay their respects to a wide range of "absent" celebrities, such as Jim Morrison, Hector Berlioz, Chopin, Sarah Bernhardt, François Truffaut, Honoré de Balzac, and Jean-Paul Sartre, all of whom are joined at last in eternity.

Which brings us to the Ile-de-France, heart of the nation, favored by nature and by history. The countryside is fertile and residents can stroll or hike through magnificent forests, like that of Fontainebleau. Here too, Gothic cathedrals and splendid châteaux dot the landscape. But the pride of Ile-de-France is certainly Paris and her greater metropolitan area, home to ten million. The statistics of the French census tell us that one in every five Frenchmen is Parisian, by birth or by residence. And the city's population continues to grow, burgeoning with new arrivals from all over France and from the rest of the world. Few of those who arrive in Paris, nowadays, come in search of artistic fame. Things were quite different at the turn of the century — then Paris lured countless young men and women questing after glory, bartering drawings and finished paintings for canvas, paint, and a bottle of absinthe, according to the lore of Bohemian legend. Pablo Picasso, Modigliani, Utrillo, and Léger lived in this picturesque Paris between the world wars. Still other young artists, their names long forgotten, experienced the same privations and endured the same poverty, but never savored the heady wine of fame and wealth.

Though not all Parisians are starving artists or penniless poets, there were times when Paris suffered great poverty; nineteenth-century novelists Emile Zola and Victor Hugo describe a city of widespread hunger and misery. Even amidst severe want, the Parisians have always worked hard to enjoy themselves, lavishing imagination and creativity on the pursuit of good times. Drawings and canvases by Degas and Toulouse Lautrec depict the cheerful atmosphere of the "cafés-concerts" and country dances of the Belle Époque. Nowadays, too, the French and foreign tourists can still enjoy the city's charm, strolling idly through the narrow streets of the Marais, sitting down to a drink in a café-théâtre in the French quarter while listening to a French comic or a jazz band, lolling at a "terrasse" along the Boulevard Saint-Germain, or promenading through the Luxembourg Gardens. Even though Paris works hard to keep the straight and serious face of a cultural and professional capital, she sets aside her most beautiful clefts and corners for sweet laziness! There are so many faces of Paris; tourists may amble off to the Lido or to the Crazy Horse Saloon, to admire the marmoreal beauty of the dancers. Hints of the Parisian gaiety celebrated by Edith Piaf can still be found along the banks of the Seine. The rows of green bookstalls attract crowds of amateur browsers and serious collectors, who stand enthralled by a first edition, an old engraving, a sepia photograph, or a tattered postcard, complete with address, message, and postmarked stamp; nearby, in Place Saint-Michel, comics and musicians attract crowds. Paris maintains her reputation — often amplified and exaggerated by the media — for elegant rendez-vous at the racetracks of Auteuil or Longchamp, for impressive official ceremonies on the Champs-Elysées, for spectacular haute-couture fashion shows or for the showings of artists in Place du Tertre. This is the flashy, traditional Paris of the postcards.

The real charm of Paris lies elsewhere however. It can be found in the heart of an old neighborhood, the intimate elegance of a gesture, the tireless labor of craftsmen and artisans: the silent work of cabinet makers in the Marais, the ceaseless shuffling patter of silk ballet slippers rehearsing *pas de deux* and *arabesques* at the Opéra, the lush and almost enchanted gardens tucked away behind the sober facades of "hôtels particuliers," the stores with antique signboards, the vendors in the vast and sprawling flea markets — these are just a few of the hidden and often-overlooked faces of this infinitely fascinating city. With patience and dedication, each and every visitor can discover this secret garden in the heart of Paris.

The Ile-de-France is not limited to Paris. The capital is surrounded by a constellation of châteaux, each of them unique and charming. To name just a few, Fontainbleau, Vaux-le-Vicomte, Versailles, each of which possesses a sumptuous garden designed by Le Nôtre. These châteaux are architectural treasures in their own right; they are, moreover, brimful of magnificent masterpieces.

The true cornucopia of spectacular châteaux, however, is Touraine and the central stretch of the Loire river valley. If Burgundy is the heart of French Romanesque, and Normandy is unrivalled for its Gothic spires and flying buttresses, this fertile valley has shown the world the epitome of Renaissance style. Amboise, Chambord, Chenonceaux, Azay-le-Rideau,

20 *These gently rolling waves at sunset, along the Basque coastline, are unusually pacific. Usually, the waves break with violence, and surfers zigzag merrily across the foamy mountains of water.*

21 top *The port of the small seaside resort of Cancale enjoys a particularly privileged view, looking out as it does on the bay of Mont-Saint-Michel and the marshlands of Dol. Located just a few miles from the fortified village of Saint-Malo, this is a must for tourists who wish to see the real Brittany.*

21 *middle and bottom. Certain unspoiled stretches of the Breton coastline evoke the times when the Celts named this region "Armorique," or "Land of the Sea." The ancient legends of this area still tinge it with a haunted air of mystery.*

22-23 *The great beach of Biarritz, southernmost point on France's Atlantic coastline, enjoys a privileged location along the sandy and irregular shore. It became the favorite resort of European nobility when the Empress Eugénie chose to winter here, with all her court, in what is now the Hôtel du Palais.*

Blois, Chinon... each of these names corresponds to a château, where visitors can follow expert guides or learn from scholarly conservators; during the summer, they can enjoy the sound-and-light shows — "spectacles son et lumière."

French poets have described the nation's rivers as routes for the conveyance of ideas as well as of freight. This poetic conceit was meant to underscore the venerable role, eminently solid after centuries of history, that the rivers of France continue to play in the life of the nation. Each region is organized around its chief river, and it is the leisurely flow of the river that sets the pace of life and change in small towns and villages. The Canal de la Marne au Rhine and the Canal du Rhône au Rhine join up with the Rhine in Strasbourg, on the Alsatian border, bone of contention and first victim in both world wars. In an irony of history, Strasbourg has now been declared the capital of Europe. For the past decade, the European parliament has held regular sessions here; when the parliament is sitting, the town is swept by unfamiliar bustle and activity. During the rest of the year, it remains a town of exquisitely provincial charm, with handsome half-beamed houses.

The wines of Alsace — Riesling, Tokay, and Sylvaner — enjoy excellent reputations, and are the product of a great tradition in the vintner's art. The orderly rows of the vineyards contrast sharply with the unruly exuberance of the century-old chestnuts, the beech trees, and the spruce pines; the trees become thicker in a riot of foliage as one enters the great Vosges forest. The traditional wine fairs offer an opportunity to show off the picturesque regional outfits, as are the folk festivals which reach some sort of Dionysian crescendo in the first week of September, when the wine spurts from the village fountain. In Colmar, a huge festival takes place in late August; the women dress in traditional garb and join the vintners to savor the succulent "choucroutes" (sauerkraut) and to sample the excellent Tokay.

Now let us leave Alsace and move on to Champagne. On the banks of the Seine, the town of Troyes boasts an amazing profusion of religious masterpieces in Gothic and Renaissance style. It is the champagne, however, and not the artworks, that has made the place famous. It is said that a certain Dom Pérignon, a monk and the master of the wine cellars at the Abbey of Hautvillers in the late seventeenth century, was the inventor of what we now call champagne, but it was not until the following century that champagne acquired its official titles of nobility.

Along the banks of the Marne, one can stumble upon sanctuaries of champagne, one after

another: Taittinger, Pommery, Lanson, Veuve Cliquot, Ruinart, and Piper-Heidsieck, and their vineyards, set off by granite markers or else enclosed behind walls. The geometric order of the vines sheers off and overlaps, mingling colors as in an Impressionist painting. This bright, sunny image, however, contrasts with the dark, subterranean world, branching off into thousands of ancient tunnels; here 600 million bottles are stored, lovingly guarded and protected from light and noise. If they were lined up, these tunnels in Reims and Épernay would stretch for nearly 200 miles. Great care and devotion are lavished, without regard for cost, in the maintenance of this stone treasurehouse where, at a constant temperature (between 8 and 12 degrees Celsius), the wines of Champagne gradually acquire all of their highly prized qualities. Much like in Alsace, this kingdom of vineyards, with its impeccable rows of trellises, contrasts sharply with the anarchy of the luxuriant forest. Grape stalks and tendrils give way to oaks, spruce trees, and beeches in the national Parc de la Montagne of Reims, one of France's sixty-three national wildlife preserves. Visitors can enjoy guided "photo-safaris," rock-climbing, skiing, hiking, and exploring in the numerous caves and grottoes, featuring amazing limestone formations. In southern France, the emerald-green triangle between the Vézère and the Dordogne river valleys is dotted with twenty-five grottoes, inhabited in prehistoric times, and with thousands of relics that speak of the presence of humans since the dawn of time. In particular, this is where the skeleton of Cro-Magnon man was unearthed, early Homo Sapiens who walked 30,000 years ago. The best-known sites are Les Eyzies, La Madeleine and, of course, the caves of Lascaux, where the earliest European humans painted astonishing works of cave art.

The French mountain chains, chief among them the Alps, the Pyrenees, and the Jura, are much frequented by nature lovers and by skiers. The winter sports complexes are extremely modern and boast thousands of chairlifts, skilifts, and funiculars, and — here and there — "ecomuseums" which provide information on the mountain paths.

Every region in France possesses its own unique features. To get to know them, one must leave the cities and towns and plunge into the countryside. An exploration of the most recondite corners of Provence, for instance, could begin in the east, where the torrential waters of the Verdon tumble through rocky gorges, or else floating down the waters of the Rhône to the delta, which spreads out through the marshlands of the Camargue. There, one finds a

23

remarkable array of fauna: beavers and badgers, but also herons and pink flamingoes, wild ducks, teals, woodcocks, aigrettes, and others. There are wild white horses and savage black bulls. The landscape of reeds and wild rose is dotted, here and there, by small whitewashed cottages, with straw roofs and huge stables — "les cabanes." These peaceful houses glitter in the sunlight, reflecting a distinctly Provencal light that appears in the work of some of the great artists of the past century — Matisse, Dufy, Gauguin, Cézanne, Picasso, Kandinsky... The people of Provence have fine-honed features, a clear mark of the hard labor involved in farming and herding. In Saint-Martin-de-la-Crau, a folk tradition still survives, involving the "gardians," local cowboys, and vast herds of sheep; there is a festival on the day that the "gardians" take leave of the village and set off for the high pastures. Scarves and felt hats are proudly shown off, as they have been for centuries, during the religious service in which man and beast receive benediction; the festival reaches a climax when the herds of sheep, hesitantly bleating, are driven off through the narrow and intricate lanes of the village and up to the hills.

On the 24th and 25th of May, the town of Saintes-Maries-de-la-Mer comes to life as a remarkable group of individuals descend upon it. There are Gitanos, Zingari, Gitanes, Sintoes, Rom, Hungarian Gypsies, Adels, Manouches and they come from all over to worship, with pagan and Christian rites, the arrival in this region of Saint Mary Jacobé, Saint Mary Salomé, and Saint Sarah-la-Kali, who was their servant, who arrived in the region around the first century A.D., according to legend. Today, the "Pilgrims of moonlight," as they are known, dance to the skittish rhythm of flamenco for two days without a break, and sing, in hoarse and mournful voices, around a bonfire. They end the celebration by solemnly walking in procession to the sea, where the "Three Marys" supposedly disembarked, in flight from persecution in Jerusalem. Provence differs from other regions both in terms of language and history. The Langue d'Oc, the original language of Provence, has been supplanted by the Langue d'Oïl, imposed by Paris, but Provençal dialect is still spoken. In historical terms, Provence differs sharply from the rest of France as well. In the first century B.C., Provence was the only Roman province in Gallic territory, and therefore it boasts many vestiges of Roman civilization.

In Orange, one can admire the splendid triumphal arch built by Julius Caesar and the perfectly preserved Roman theater, which contains an imposing statue of Augustus, sixteen feet high. Here, as in the

24-25 At the Rhône delta, where the river's twin streams meet the sea, there stretches a wild land, odorous with tamarisks, abounding in extraordinary flora (salicorne, saladelle) and fauna (beavers, herons, pink flamingoes, aigrettes, wild ducks...). Here too one finds white horses and black bulls, tall rushes and

colorful wild roses, plentiful fishing and salt marshes. There is another, agrarian Camargue, a region of vast landholdings, sheep herding, vineyards, legumes, forage, and rice.

26-27 *The little Corsican town of Saint-Florent lies at the end of a gulf, on the north of the island, surrounded by groves of olive trees with twisted shapes, orderly vineyards, and fruit orchards, typical of the region. One can stroll and pass the time of day here very agreeably, along the marina and through the old town, clustered around the church, under the sheltering walls of the ancient Genoese citadel.*

arena in nearby Arles, these ancient theaters host performances of modern times, whether it be opera or bloody bullfights. The birth of civilization in this region dates back even further, to circa 600 B.C., when Greeks from Asia Minor founded Marseille and discovered the beauty of such coastal sites as Nice, Antibes, and Cannes. Successive cultures left marks of their glory on this land troubled by the mistral, the rough north wind: in the white ruins of Glanum, in the Avignon of the pontiffs, and in fortified inland villages. Craftsmanship vaunts a very ancient tradition, as in the manufacture of the "santons" of Provence, or the pottery of Vallauris, already well known during the reign of the Roman emperor Tiberius — these ceramic creations enjoyed new popularity thanks to the innovations of Picasso.

In the sixteenth century, in Grasse, Catherine de' Médici encouraged the distillation of fragrant perfumes and essences, today an important category in the French economy and a fundamental feature of French charm. Visitors to this remarkable land will find their needs cared for, by a sophisticated industry of hospitality, and by the natural generosity of the people. Artists in search of solitude and concentration have rediscovered the long-forgotten mountain villages, often called "eagles' nests." These delightful eyries are not frequented by mass tourism, because they are so hard to reach, although they are often close to the coast. South of Marseille, "calanques," steep and jagged inlets, provide natural harbor for pleasure boats.

The international jet set may prevail on the Promenade des Anglais in Nice or along La Croisette in Cannes; the Basque coast, in contrast, still offers the refined style of the nineteenth-century aristocracy. Once, empresses, archdukes, and princesses met there to spend the winter and to enjoy the Atlantic setting; they stayed in luxurious hotels with stunning views of the Grande-Plage, the great beach, and they squandered immense fortunes on the green felt gaming tables of the Casino Bellevue. These days, those waves crash near vacationers engaging in more athletic forms of entertainment - the crowned heads of Europe have made way for those modern acrobats, the surfers. Biarritz has become the European capital of this sport. And there is another, equally important sport, that has conquered the Basques - golf. The lush green golf courses that extend in all directions would almost lead one to believe that golf has replaced pelota - a version of jai alai or handball - as the local sport. That's not quite true of course; every town and village boasts a pelota court, where the feverish game is played with a

small fast ball made of sheepskin and fleece. The court usually stands beside the town hall and the parish church, with its distinctive engraved wooden galleries. Everywhere are white houses, decorated with sky blue paint, and with wooden beams painted bright green and red. The restaurants are charming; garish tablecloths are spread upon great tables made of rough, dark wood. Huge fireplaces and bunches of red peppers adorn the walls; the peppers can be found in almost every Basque dish.

Solid respect for local traditions dictates the menu; a typical meal might call fo"piperade" (scrambled eggs and ham), with such light wines as Irouléguy. Banquets and weddings are often enlivened with spectacular folk dances, to the joy of the tourists. The Basque language is still spoken; its roots have never been successfully traced, and no other languages are quite like it. Every French region along a border, after all, boasts greater idiosyncrasies than the other, inland regions; Corsica is perhaps the most extreme example of this rule, reinforced by its island nature.

Perhaps the most remarkable feature of Corsica is the rapidity with which one can shift from the snows of Cinto to the palm trees of Ajaccio, from the savage arena of Spelunca to the beautiful gulf of Porto, from the cool forests of Vizzavona to the scorching desert of Agriates. The island boasts torrential streams, high mountain lakes, alpine meadows and dark chestnut groves, odorous heather and towering pines, rocky inlets with bloody-red boulders and chalk cliffs plunging into the sea. At Bonifacio, the cliffs rear 200 feet above the waves. Some scholars say that Homer set a scene in the tenth book of the Odyssey, in which Ulysses combats mythical giants, in this natural harbor encircled by boulders. And the challenge of adventure is always available to those modern Ulysses who wish to explore the towns and inlets of this Island of Beauty. And so are Saint-Malo, Reims, Poitier, Honfleur, Nancy, Dinan, Carcassonne, Orléans... and so many other places that *la douce France* can be considered an infinite resource.

A perfect hexagon

The natural plenty of the French soil is an integral part of our imagery, and paintings spread the image as well, transfigured in *en plein air* by Monet, precise and neat in *pointillisme* by Seurat, or reinvented by Van Gogh's visionary soul. But impressionist talent has been perhaps more faithful to reality than the green, purple, and blue reveal. The French countryside is always waiting for acute observers to depict its landscape.

The hexagonal shape of France almost seems to have been planned at a drawing board, in the most logical fashion possible. The country is perfectly symmetrical — three continental and three maritime "facets"; one facet washed by the Atlantic, one by the Mediterranean, and the last on the English Channel. In the middle is the Massif Central. From the steep gorges of the Verdon, with vertical drops of two thousand feet, to the volcanic cones of Auvergne, from the high Norman cliffs of Dieppe, wet with the foam of the crashing rollers of the Channel, to the sun-kissed beaches of the Côte d'Azur, the visitor can explore an incessantly changing landscape; few can claim to know this country well.

28 top The Monts du Morvan have been protected by the creation in 1970 of a regional wildlife park. Set in the heart of Burgundy, the area is dotted with lakes which glitter in the forested landscape.

28 bottom The Auvergne is a region of outstanding beauty, a lake district with a splendid landscape. This view of a dramatic boulder crowned by a medieval abbey is not unique in this area.

29 The luxuriant Dordogne Valley boasts the splendid Château of Beynac, built in medieval times. Here, landscapes are still unspoiled; rivers wend across the landscape, and at each curve of the stream one sees a château or a church, like so many stone sentinels.

Country landscapes

30 *The château of Jumilhac looms over the surrounding valley, its typical military architecture adorned by handsome corner turrets and slate roofs.*

Haute-Provence presents sunny and winding landscapes with wooded hills and rock spurs emerging from a uniform, green plain where history has left memories of ancient civilizations in the many Roman sites and in strongholds like Jomilhac. This area claims primacy for the production of lavender, which permeates the air with its fragrance, together with the aromas of thyme and other herbs growing wild on the side of the nearby mountains. The enterprising citizens of Digne have dedicated an annual event to the "market" of lavender, from August to September, when the mistral blows through the valleys and takes everything apart. Provence is the region that has the widest variety of landscapes, as its northern limits are the snow-capped calcareous mountains, and the southern ones the sandy beaches of the Mediterranean. Although it appears to be a contradiction, inland and coastal areas share a common characteristic – a brightness which has fans worldwide and which makes the territory one of the main destinations for tourists. Nearly all modern artistic trends have been influenced by this brightness through the commitment of Cézanne, Picasso, Matisse, Signac, Monet, Le Corbusier, and Van Gogh.

31 *Solemn and imposing, an alpine range stands high above the bright landscape of Haute-Provence. Tilled fields alternate with somber scrublands, and here and there stands a small village, dotted with quaint pointed roofs, set on a gentle slope in a serene setting.*

Wine-growing regions

The French landscape is never dull —
and the products of that landscape are
as varied and surprising as the
landscape itself. The visitor can
sample a seemingly infinite range of
wines, savoring the craft of the
vintner, yet clearly detecting the
original, pristine qualities of the fruit.
Sparkling and refined champagne —
from the region of the same name —
the full-bodied red wines of
Burgundy, the well known Côtes-du-
Rhône and the agreeable white wines
of Alsace, the universe of French
wines offers something for every
palate. The masters of this precious
nectar devote endless care and
attention to its creation; French wine
rightly claims a place of honor in the
cultural and artistic heritage of each
region. These trellised vines bear
witness to the effort and devotion
lavished to maintain a pleasing order
in terrace and hillside; that devotion
pays off in the finished product. And
tourists can sample that product in a
tour of the vineyards and vintners,
open to the public.

*34-35 Champagne is grown in three
"départements." Most of the grapes (80
per cent) grown here are used in
making champagne .*

Brittany

The Breton region abounds in things to see and places to go; visitors are enthralled by the artistic and natural treasures, as well as by the intriguing character of the Bretons. The distinctive personality of the inhabitants is perhaps a result of daily exposure to the rage and exuberance of the Atlantic Ocean; the elements have endowed the Bretons with a spirit of tenacity and determination. In the Bretons, strong religious faith combines with the stout Celtic soul; the result of this unusual alchemy is a popular imagination capable of concocting surreal and fantastic legends and myths. Thus, this region is the homeland of the Holy Grail and of Tristan and Isolde, whose story inspired Wagner's opera. The visitor can indulge in romantic reveries on the "actual" site of the legendary events. It is, in fact, possible to follow a route — parallel to tours of actual historical sites — of legendary sites featuring the heroes and characters of Arthurian legend. This is the land of the sorcerer Merlin and of Lancelot du Lac, as much as it is the land of the megalithic monuments of Carnac and Menec, or of the unsettling carved stone calvaries which date from the Middle Ages.

36-37 Small harbors crowded with boats, fishermen's watering holes with signs corroded by salt air, castles girt by ramparts and surrounding by close-pressed homes — these are just a few aspects of ordinary Breton life.

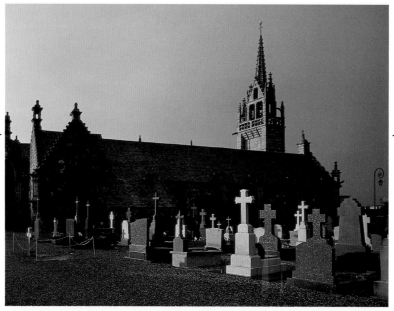

To live by the breath of the tide

38 top *The Church of Guimiliau in Brittany. In many Breton villages, artists and craftsmen have found concrete expression for the religious feelings of the inhabitants through "calvaries," abounding in real and allegorical characters, displayed in the "enclos paroissiaux" or in countless churches and chapels.*

38 bottom *Wind and sea savage the jagged shoreline of a bay that has earned for itself the unsettling name of "Baie des Trépassés," or "Bay of the Dead."*

39 top *This home in the seaside resort of Quiberon is set on the far tip of the peninsula. The slow work of time and the ocean has linked this strip of granite to the mainland; Quiberon is now a major tourist attraction.*

39 bottom *The coastline of the peninsula of Quiberon is also called "Côte Sauvage," because of its harsh and daunting appearance.*

Living in time with the ocean

The photographs on these two pages show everyday life in Honfleur; this is just one of the many facets of life in Normandy. For the region is also a vast farmland, dotted with small neat fields, dairy farms, and endless rows of apple trees, which yield the excellent Norman cider. Normandy also abounds in venerable abbeys, châteaux, and manors, often described by Gustave Flaubert and Guy de Maupassant.

42-43 *Mont-Saint-Michel is unlike anything else on earth. Set amidst an expanse of ever-changing sands which are illuminated by the restless coastal light and flooded at regular intervals by the most powerful tides in Europe, the island-abbey rears up, a startling metaphor for medieval society.*

44-45 *Those who first see Normandy from the sea are astonished at the white expanse of the cliffs of Étretat; this huge geological formation is mirrored in the cobalt waters in an endless series of reflections.*

46-47 *This is a night-time view of the old port of La Rochelle; among the town's many towers, the Tour de la Chaine, as its name suggests, bears witness to the medieval custom of closing the port with a great chain, at night and in times of danger.*

Where space expands in silence and solitude

48 *The region of Queyras abounds in attractions, both in winter and summer; the Guil valley is especially interesting, and lies in the shadow of Monviso, the summit of which is in Italy.*

49 *The French Alps attract millions of visitors who want to enjoy the unforgettable landscapes and relax mind and body with healthy sporting activities. From Briançon, the visitor can enjoy a wide variety of activities; the Parc National des Écrins, seen here, is close by.*

50-51 *The border between France and Italy crosses the snow-covered peak of Mont Blanc; each year, groups of intrepid mountain climbers reach the peak. This feat, first accomplished in 1786, requires great experience and the assistance of a guide.*

At the foot of the highest mountain in the Alps, Mont Blanc, lies the town of Chamonix; the vast glacier of Bossons separates the village from the peak, which glitters with thousands of crystal facets. As in so many other Alpine stations, an ancient village lies at the heart of Chamonix; around it, modern sport facilities, hotels, swimming pools, and restaurants have sprung up, and are now patronized by a sophisticated international clientele. A tunnel approximately eight miles long connects Chamonix to Courmayeur on the Italian side. For those who prefer to sway in high winds at great height, a funicular connects the town to Entrèves — also on the Italian side — the cables pass over snowfields and glaciers, all the way up to Helbronner Point. From there, there is a gentle descent to Val d'Aoste; passengers can enjoy breathtaking panoramas and dizzying views of sheer drops. The ski slopes of Chamonix swarm with an army of skiers, attracted by the pure air and the amazing views. At some distance from the bustling heart of the town, one can still find small chapels, ancient chalets, and — in the springtime — fields full of wildflowers, shrouded in a profound, all-enveloping silence.

54-55 *The Pyrenees stretch from the Atlantic Ocean to the Mediterranean Sea. Their valleys descend northward, creating a number of mountainous realms. These narrow lands are linked by high passes, whose names — and steepness — are well known to the competitors of the Tour de France bicycle race.*

The Mediterranean coast

56-57 *The Côte d'Azur has changed radically in the past few decades. The ancient fishing villages are gone without a trace; the entire coastline is falling prey to real estate developers. Cannes (top left), Nice (bottom left), and Saint Tropez (right) are internationally renowned resorts.*

58-59 *Near Cassis, the Mediterranean coastline is broken by "calanques," jagged narrow bays, marked by steep rocky shores.*

Mediterranean islands

In forgotten eras, the Maures mountain chain extended into the Mediterranean; the Hyères islands formed part of the chain, and then gradually broke off, over the eons. Porquerolles Island, back then, was covered with luxuriant pine forests, eucalyptus trees, heather, and myrtle. Although the island was swept by brush fires in the last century, and its vegetation was decimated, it still preserves a savage beauty.

Corsica

Corsica was occupied, in turn, by the Iberians, the Ligurians, the Etruscans, the Carthaginians — all these people settled and fought here. Then came the Romans' turn; the Empire used the island as a place of banishment, and, according to legend, the philosopher Seneca languished here for several years as a prisoner. The Byzantines were the next lords of the island, followed by Franks, Saracens, and most recently, the Genoese, under whom the island enjoyed five centuries of relative stability. The Genoese overlordship came to an end in 1789, when Corsica became French. It is separated into two "départements" — Haute-Corse and Corse-du-Sud, it now enjoys partial political independence.

Just as the island's history is a varied succession of different peoples, so too is Corsica's physical appearance always surprising, never dull. A mountain chain — reaching an altitude of around 9,000 feet at the peak of Mount Cinto — crosses the island from north to south; here one can ski and enjoy other winter sports. The island's valleys are shaded by forests and underbrush, and in places vineyards grow, and fields of flowers scent the air. The coastline is a succession of narrow, rocky inlets with pink granite walls, surveyed by venerable watchtowers, white cliffs, pleasant bays, and tiny colorful harbor towns. The eastern section of the island is flat and covered with marshy plains. The mainland French seem to love Corsica; in the Sixties, French vacationers began to abandon the hustle-bustle of the Côte d'Azur in favor of this tropical island paradise.

64 The island of Lavezzi, south of Corsica, abounds in rocks of all sizes. The limpid waters are ideal, however, for snorkeling and scuba diving, and just plain swimming.

65 This photograph was taken near Bonifacio; set among steep white cliffs, the Pertusato lighthouse can be seen.

66-67 The small town of Bonifacio, built on a cliff 200 feet above sea level, catches the last rays of evening sunlight.

The lessons of life

France is generally considered a land where people know how to live well. What is the secret of this enviable French reputation? For this country is changing as fast as any other, and transition threatens the French style of life. Nonetheless, at the time of writing, the French are defending — with resounding success — their style and quality of life, so much a part of the country's identity.

France is everywhere known as the country of *savoir vivre*, where a light nonchalance is exalted as a philosophy of life and where the secret of a happy life seems to have its origin, considering the overmentioned *joie de vivre*. But what then is the formula that gave so many flattering and positive commonplaces to the French people? Perhaps the quality of life is proportional to the human dimension, which everywhere degenerates too much in huge suburbs, chaotic highways, and enormous factories. Paris is the only French metropolis and, together with the Ile-de-France, includes almost one-fifth of the entire national population.

The urbanization, except for the capital, is not very accentuated, so this country continues to be represented by a region marked by various and rich cultures reflecting local customs. Based on these presuppositions of equilibrium, France will go on avoiding standardization and exporting important things . . . haute couture, haute cuisine . . . remaining a symbol of refinement.

68-69 A chat and a bite at a local café seems to be a fundamental ingredient in a Parisian day. The tables are set outdoors in the summer, behind glass in the winter.

Parisian charm

The café is a fundamental feature of Parisian life. Oddly, the first café was not founded by a Frenchman, but by a Sicilian, a certain Procopio dei Costelli, who gave a French version of his name to his establishment — Le Procope. Located in Rue de l'Ancienne-Comédie, this café soon became the meeting place for Parisian artists. Literary and political generations followed one after the other — Voltaire, d'Alembert, and Diderot, and then the Romantics, lastly Gambetta and his journalist friends. Toward the end of the last century, the café became, once again, an exquisitely literary realm, with Paul Verlaine and company.

72-73 The terrace of the Restaurant Grande Cascade, in the Bois de Boulogne.

74-75 Twice yearly, Paris hosts the fashion shows of French haute couture. Each fashion house (Lacroix, Saint Laurent, Dior, Chanel) presents the newest creations. The audience, made up for the most part of fashion journalists and professionals, is demanding and influential.

71

Legends à la carte

French cuisine is world renowned, both for its quality and for the variety of dishes. Here food is an art, a philosophy, even a religion, with great chefs as high priests and fine restaurants as temples in which the ritual secrets are jealously preserved. Classic French cuisine requires time and devotion to detail, along with such fresh and delicate ingredients as truffles, mushrooms, cognac, butter,

78-79 Cognac is distilled — and redistilled — from wine made from "folle-blanche" grapes; the distilling process follows methods and uses equipment that date back over the centuries. This picture perfectly depicts the patient labor of the craftsmen who make cognac, amidst hundreds of oaken barrels — a candle is used to warm the liquid prior to tasting.

and cream. Herbs and spices are skilfully blended into exquisite sauces. Nouvelle cuisine, fashionable in recent years, calls for a simpler approach to sauces and condiments, and emphasizes the natural flavors of the ingredients. Local cuisines are also greatly prized. The construction of Paris's great boulevards engendered the establishment of the city's great restaurants, and in them one can often see original decor from that period: at the Tour d'Argent, one can sit by large windows and look out at the apse of Notre-Dame; at Le Grand Véfour, one can sit where Napoleon Bonaparte or Jean Cocteau once dined.

Ancient
traditions

80-81 *Around the world, late summer is harvest time. But for farmers in the Deux-Sèvres area, machinery has not entirely replaced the traditional methods.*

82-83 *By virtue of its fertile soil, the Vaucluse produces particularly savory fruit and vegetables, much sought after by the great chefs of nouvelle cuisine.*

At La Garette or at Coulon, visitors can rent a boat to tour the Parc Naturel du Marais Poitevin, one of the largest in France, extending over 60,000 hectares in area. There are two types of "marais" — the wetlands variety, extending from Niort to Damvix (15,000 hectares), which has been dubbed the "Green Venice," with an intricate network of channels running under a canopy of poplars and beeches. This sort of "marais" is devoted to horticulture, and one can only get around by boat. There is another kind, the "dry marais" (40,000 hectares); this "marais" is also crisscrossed by drainage canals, but cattle are grazed here.

Oysters,
a delicacy
from the sea

Oysters are fished heavily off the Channel and Atlantic coasts. In the Gulf of Morbihan, especially, oysters are caught in the following manner: baby oysters (they are usually 1/3 mm in size) which float with the currents attach themselves to the nets set out for this purpose. After eight months, the oysters are removed and placed in oyster farms. When they attain the right size, after two or three years, they are removed and shipped to special oyster plants where another year goes by before they are ready to eat.

88-89 *Oyster harvest on the Norman coast.*

Dance and costume

In France, each region possesses a traditional costume. Of course, the costumes are rarely worn nowadays, but they are shown off with pride during festivals. The most remarkable costumes are those of Alsace, Brittany — with lovely lace headgear — and the Pays Basque. The costumes of Arles are described at length in the works of Alphonse Daudet and Frédéric Mistral.

Passion on horseback

The "gardians" of the Camargue have become legendary for their skill in breaking wild horses and fierce bulls. In this land, among ponds and marshes, white horses live practically wild, alongside black bulls that are dangerous to approach — ever ready to charge at careless tourists. Great care is required to transport these animals to the corridas in Arles or Nîmes, where they are sacrificed to the applause of the public, who are seated on the stone steps of ancient Roman arenas. Lassoed and haltered, their horns padded to protect them during transport, the bulls are loaded onto special vehicles. Transporting cows is no less complicated; they are a source of considerable concern to the "gardians" because they are quite agile, and sometimes leap over the sides of the arena, causing the spectators to scatter. Aside from bullfights, the Provençals are fond of other forms of sport with bulls, often less bloody. In the famed "course à la cocarde," for instance, young men snatch a ribbon set between the horns of the bull.

In search of history

Each part of France boasts architectural treasures, whether they be Romanesque churches, Gothic cathedrals, or châteaux dating from the Renaissance or later; there are fortified towns and entire neighborhoods that have preserved the same appearance for centuries.

Here each historical stage is displayed with an abundance of temples, palaces, castles, and cathedrals, in a millenarian carousel involving the capital as well as the farthest province. The driving force of such vast initiative is certainly due to the richness of genial minds, but also and above all else to the "grandeur" which has promoted titanic achievements for nationalistic conceit and desire for eternity. Time has never stopped; rather, it appears to have chosen a committing challenge to anticipate the aesthetic/architectural dictates of the coming century. The near future has been already overlapped by the inspiration of the Défense district on the Paris outskirts, by the holiday center "La Grande Motte" on the Languedoc coast, or by the Pompidou centre. In France, perhaps, someone is already designing the 22nd century.

94 top *The great avenue of the Champs-Elysées intersects with the Place de l'Etoile, where twelve main streets lead away from the monumental Arc de Triomphe.*

94 below *The Moulin Rouge and Place Pigalle have been the regular meeting places of Paris's nightowls for many generations.*

95 *The Eiffel Tower, now over a century old, was completed in 1889. It is more than 900 feet tall.*

The city
of light

96 left *The white cupola of Sacré-Coeur, a basilica that surveys all of Paris from atop Montmartre. From the lantern, visitors can enjoy a splendid panorama.*

96 right *Le Café des Deux Magots, in Saint-Germain-des-Prés, became famous in the Fifties when it was chosen as a favorite meeting place by the French Existentialists. It has always been a popular Parisian rendezvous.*

97 *Not far from the Opéra, in the ninth arrondissement, is the Galeries Lafayette, a world-famous Parisian department store.*

98-99 *A singular view of île de la Cité, with a close-up of Notre-Dame cathedral and its renowned spire.*

99 *The Louvre boasts remarkable collections of Egyptian, Greek, and Roman art; its reputation is based, however, on the collection of paintings.*

Silk spinner
to the king

Lyon is France's second-largest city. Built at the foot of a hill, at the confluence of the rivers Saône and Rhône, Lyon is often shrouded in heavy fog. The old section of the city is the most extensive complex of Renaissance and fifteenth-century monuments to be found in France. Nothing could be more agreeable than a pleasant stroll through the Vieux-Lyon district, followed by a meal in a "bouchon," one of Lyon's typical restaurants. Lyon first became an industrial center in the sixteenth century, with the manufacture of silk. Francis I was concerned by France's volume of imported silk, and so he founded a royal manufactury, and hired expert spinners from Genoa.

Historic towns

102 top *The city of Nancy is best known for the spectacular Place Stanislas, a masterpiece of mid-eighteenth-century architecture. The cast-iron gate, chased with gold, is the work of Jean Lamour; the fountains are by the sculptor Guibal.*

102 bottom *The cathedral of Notre-Dame, in the central Place du Cardinal Luçon, overlooks the city of Reims. This Gothic masterpiece boasts majestic towers, over 270 feet tall; a rose window about 40 feet across in the western facade; and fine statues that adorn the portals.*

103 *In the heart of the old section of Rouen, where automobiles are forbidden, pedestrians walk under the Gros-Horloge, an arch with a giant clock dial facing in either direction. The clockworks date from 1389.*

104-105 *At the confluence of the Ille and the Rhine, and crisscrossed by the canals that connect the two rivers, Strasbourg lives at two radically different speeds. The city is at once a major European metropolis and a venerable and charming Alsatian provincial town.*

106-107 *The original plan of Marseille was based on a perpendicular grid of streets; the best known artery is the Canebière, which leads down to the old waterfront, the "Vieux Port." Along its banks, there are a number of bistrots and restaurants serving the local speciality, bouillabaisse.*

The deathless relics of Roman civilization

108 top *The Roman amphitheater in Orange, the wall behind the stage still intact.*

108 bottom *The bridge at Avignon, built in the twelfth century.*

108-109 *The Roman amphitheater at Arles, built in the first century A.D., was used as a fortress in the Middle Ages; hence the three watchtowers.*

110-111 *The fortified medieval village of Aigues-Mortes lies just west of the Camargue.*

In the heart of Languedoc

An ancient Roman fortress, built on the foothills of the Pyrenees, Carcassonne was expanded by the Visigoths. After the Franks took over, the town continued to grow until the thirteenth century, when it was completely surrounded by walls. The river Aude separates the Ville Basse, or "low town," from the Cité, or city center, with the most remarkable set of medieval walls in Europe. The entire complex is in a perfect state of conservation, largely due to the complete restoration performed a century ago by the architect Viollet-le-Duc.

114-115 In Vaucluse, not far from Cavaillon, a small and remote valley protects the abbey of Sénanque, founded in 1148 by Cistercian monks. Cloister and church are intact; they are now used as a cultural center; during the summer, a festival of medieval music is held here — a more suitable setting could not be imagined.

A prayer in stone and glass

Work began on the cathedral of Chartres in 1194. This church offered a second birth to Gothic architecture. The building is remarkably homogeneous, chiefly because its construction spanned no more than three decades; it served as a classic model for the cathedrals built in later years in Reims and Amiens. The choir of Chartres, larger than any other, and the immense transept, designed to accommodate vast throngs, seem to have been built in order to allow the pilgrims to gather as close as possible to the holy altar. This is a building of the people, in which burghers, peasants, and craftsmen vied with princes in their generosity, devotion, and in the honor of placing their coat of arms or that of their guild in the stained glass, in eternal commemoration.

The Palace of the Sun King

Where Versailles now stands, when Louis XIV took the throne, there was nothing more than a hunting lodge. The king quickly decided that some changes were in order. He "stole" the team of architects and artists that his finance minister, Nicolas Fouquet, had employed to build Vaux-le-Vicomte, and ordered them to embellish and expand on the existing structure. Le Brun was in charge of the buildings, while Le Nôtre oversaw the planning and decoration of the gardens. Work went on at length, as Louis XIV became increasingly ambitious, and decided to add buildings. At last, the king and his court took up residence in Versailles in 1682, while work was still proceeding. Mansart still had 36,000 soldiers and laborers on the job. Versailles is now a legend, and bears witness to the remarkable vigor of French art in the seventeenth and eighteenth centuries.

A voyage through the Renaissance

The château of Fontainebleau castle stands just southeast of Paris. Built at the wish of Francis I, it has been extensively renovated at the behest of the many sovereigns who lived in it, in accordance with the tastes and styles of their reigns: the gallery of Francis I, the ballroom of Henry II, the suites of the queen mothers Catherine and Marie de' Medici and Anne of Austria, the throne room with the Louis XIII ceiling, the suite of Madame de Maintenon, the Louis XV wing, the boudoir of Marie-Antoinette... Napoleon refurnished many of the rooms, and the Cour du Cheval Blanc (courtyard of the white horse), with its famed horse-shoe staircase, has always been the Courtyard of Farewells.

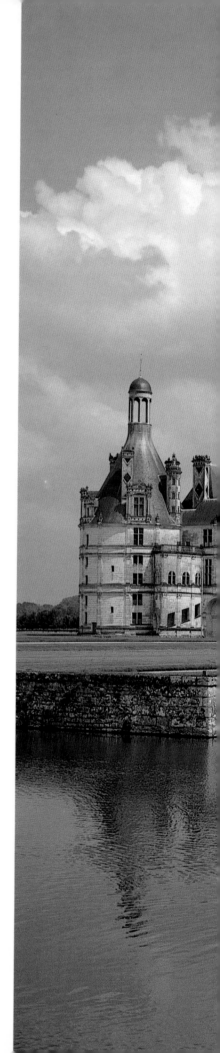

122 top *The château of Azay-le-Rideau was built on the river Indre. The corner turrets, reflected in the river, are built in the graceful style of the early French Renaissance.*

122 bottom *The château of Moulin was built near Lassay, for Philippe du Moulin. It is made up of two buildings, mirrored in the waters of the moat.*

122-123 *The château of Chambord stands on the left bank of the Loire. Set within an enclosure, it possesses a central keep with four towers. Its distinguishing feature is the contrast between the simplicity of its facade and the welter of adornments upon the keep.*

124-125 *A wide avenue lined with plane trees leads to the bridge at the entrance of the château of Chenonceaux, surrounded by French gardens enclosed by a moat. At the rear, a long five-arch bridge topped by a gallery crosses the river Cher. In the sixteenth century it was a setting for feasts and banquets held by the court of Catherine de' Mèdici.*

126-127 *The château of Amboise, in the town where Leonardo da Vinci died in 1519, is built on a rock overlooking the Loire. It stands between two enormous round towers; the Tour des Minimes, near the Loire, could be reached on horseback due to a spiral ramp.*

Photo credits:

Marcello Bertinetti/White Star archives:
pages 7; 8-9; 26-27; 50-51; 57; 60-61;
62; 64-70; 76 left; 94 bottom; 95; 96
right.

Angela White/White Star archives:
pages 6; 63; 71-73.

Luciano Ramires: back cover;
Pages 10-13; 16-21; 24-25; 28 top; 34-
36; 38-43; 46-47; 49; 53-55; 58-59; 86-
89; 96 left; 97; 98-99; 102 top; 103;
109-111; 116-117; 118 top right; 118
bottom; 119; 120-121; 128.

Apa Photo Agency: pages 28 bottom; 44-
45; 56 bottom.

Nilo Celoria: pages 91 right; 92-93.

Anne Conway: pages 31; 76 bottom; 77;
108 top.

Dallas & John Eaton/Apa Photo Agency:
pages 104-105.

Damm/Zefa: pages 2-3; 123.

Bernard and Catherine Desjeux:
Cover ; pages 48; 80-85; 124-125.

Jean Dugest/Apa Photo Agency:
pages 14-15.

Eigen/Zefa: page 32.

Cesare Gerolimetto: pages 1; 100 left;
101.

Hackensberg/Zefa: page 122.

Simeone Huber: pages 112-115.

Dennis Lane/Apa Photo Agency: page 84
top.

Dennis Mansel/Apa Photo Agency: pages
126-127.

Christine and Jean-Charles Pinheira:
pages 4-5; 56 top; 90; 91 left; 106-107;
108 bottom.

Paul Van Riel/Apa Photo Agency: pages
74-75.

Starfoto/Zefa: page 33.

Rick Strange/Apa Photo Agency: page 52.

Stretchan/Zefa: page 37.

Angelo Tondini/Focus Team: pages 102
bottom; 118 top left.

Adina Tony/Apa Photo Agency: pages 22-
23; 29; 30.

Valentin/Hoa-Qui: page 100 right.

Zefa: pages 78-79.

Bob Zola/Overseas: page 76 top right.